Fireflies

Steven Otfinoski

Cavendish
Square

New York

Published in 2014 by Cavendish Square Publishing, LLC
303 Park Avenue South, Suite 1247, New York, NY 10010

Library of Congress Cataloging-in-Publication Data

Otfinoski, Steven.
Fireflies / by Steven Otfinoski.
p. cm. — (Backyard safari)
Includes index.
ISBN 978-1-62712-307-5 (hardcover) ISBN 978-1-62712-308-2 (paperback) ISBN 978-1-62712-309-9 (ebook)
1. Fireflies — Juvenile literature. I. Otfinoski, Steven. II. Title.
QL596.L28 084 2014
595.76—dc23

Editorial Director: Dean Miller
Senior Editor: Peter Mavrikis
Copy Editor: Cynthia Roby
Art Director: Jeffrey Talbot
Designer: Joseph Macri
Photo Researcher: Alison Morretta
Production Manager: Jennifer Ryder-Talbot
Production Editor: Andrew Coddington

The photographs in this book are used by permission and through the courtesy of: Cover photo by James Jordan Photography/Flickr/Getty Images; Clarence Holmes / age fotostock / SuperStock, 4; Glow Images, Inc/Glow/Getty Images, 5; © Degginger, Phil / Animals Animals, 7; Cathy Keifer/Shutterstock.com, 8; Biosphoto / SuperStock, 9; Steven Puetzer/Photographer's Choice/Getty Images, 10; James Jordan Photography/Flickr/Getty Images, 12; Fer Gregory/Shutterstock.com, 13; Gail Shumway/Photographer's Choice/Getty Images, 14; age fotostock / SuperStock, 15; © Lloyd, James E. / Animals Animals, 17; © Lloyd, James E. / Animals Animals, 17; Clarence Holmes / age fotostock / SuperStock, 17; © Wild & Natural / Animals Animals, 17; South12th Photography/Shutterstock.com, 18; Minden Pictures / SuperStock, 20; Gail Shumway/Photographer's Choice/Getty Images, 22; Jana Leon/Photonica/Getty Images, 25; © Degginger, Phil / Animals Animals, 26.

Printed in the United States of America

Contents

Introduction   **4**

ONE Firefly World   **5**

TWO You Are the Explorer   **10**

THREE A Guide to Fireflies   **15**

FOUR Try This! Projects You Can Do   **22**

Glossary   **28**

Find Out More   **30**

Index   **31**

Introduction

Have you ever watched baby spiders hatch from a silky egg sac? Or watched a butterfly sip nectar from a flower? If you have, you know how wonderful it is to discover nature for yourself. Each book in the Backyard Safari series takes you step-by-step on an easy outdoor adventure, then helps you identify the animals you've found. You'll also learn ways to attract, observe, and protect these valuable creatures. As you read, be on the lookout for the Safari Tips and Trek Talk facts sprinkled throughout the book. Ready? The fun starts just steps from your back door!

ONE
Firefly World

Have you ever seen fireflies light up your yard on a summer night? They look like tiny blinking stars in the darkness. Only these "stars" are close to the ground, so close you can reach out and touch them.

Fireflies, also called lightning bugs, are actually not flies at all. They aren't bugs either. They are **beetles**—insects with hard, external bodies and wings. Unlike most beetles and other insects, fireflies produce their own light.

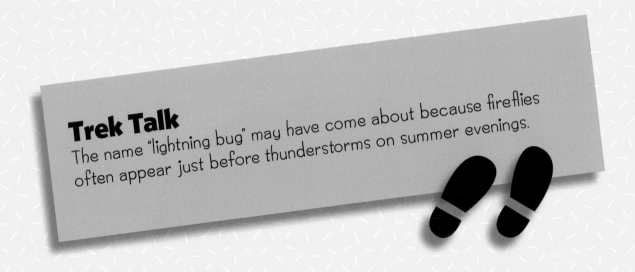

Trek Talk
The name "lightning bug" may have come about because fireflies often appear just before thunderstorms on summer evenings.

Mating Time

The glowing light made by the firefly serves an important purpose. It is a signal that helps it locate a **mate**. Male fireflies fly through the air at the first sign of dusk. They give off a blinking pattern of lights that is unique to their **species**. Females of the same firefly species rest in bushes, tree branches, and tall grass. When they see the signal of a male that they recognize, they flash the same pattern of light if they are interested. The male then lands nearby, and the two mate.

The female firefly lays its eggs in the earth or in moist areas. The eggs later hatch and become **larvae**. The larvae often glow with a light as well. The larva stage can last up to a year. Also called glowworms, larvae have big appetites. They will eat earthworms, snails, and even other insect larvae. They sting their **prey** with poison to kill it.

The larva eventually develops into a **pupa**, and from this stage it finally emerges as an adult firefly. Unlike the larva, the adult firefly has a very short life span. It will live only long enough to mate and give birth to the next generation. Its life ranges from five days to two months. During this time, the firefly may eat only the nectar of flowers, pollen, or nothing at all.

Safari Tip
Some female fireflies of one species will imitate the signal of another species. When the male of this species lands to mate, the female will attack and eat it!.

Firefly Bodies

Adult fireflies have fat, oblong hard bodies .25 to .75 inches (.75–2 cm) in length. They are usually brown or black in color with markings of orange, red, or yellow. Like most beetles, the firefly has two pairs of wings. The top pair, called the **elytra**, isn't used for flying, but is a protective cover for the wings that lie underneath it.

The firefly's light is produced by an organ located underneath its **abdomen**. A chemical reaction takes place inside this organ to produce the light, which is called **bioluminescence**. The organ takes in oxygen from the air and mixes it with a substance called luciferin and an **enzyme** called luciferase. The combination of these three substances

Trek Talk
Fireflies also use their light to warn off **predators**. It tells them that fireflies do not taste good. Their light can warn other males also looking for females to mate to stay out of their territory as well.

creates the light. A firefly's light is unique in that it produces no heat. Scientists call it a "cold light." In contrast, an incandescent bulb, the kind you might use at home, only emits 10 percent of its energy as light and the rest as heat. A fluorescent bulb, the kind used at your school, emits 90 percent of its energy as light.

The firefly's two pairs of wings can be clearly seen in this photo.

Fireflies use their light to communicate with each other. They also use their light to attract the opposite sex and mate. When you see a male firefly fluttering around in your backyard, odds are that he is trying to gain the attention of a female. The female may be more difficult to spot. Females will stay close to the ground or may even be spotted resting on a fence.

There are about 2,000 species of fireflies. They live on every continent except Antarctica. You may find them in your yard in the summer, when most fireflies are active. Keep in mind, that you will not find any fireflies if it is raining outside. Your best odds of spotting a firefly are during warm, dry evenings. Are you ready to see a firefly flashing its light? It's time to go on safari.

TWO

You Are the Explorer

Fireflies caught in a jar can give off a surprising amount of light.

Some fireflies come out in the winter months, but most can be found in summer. Begin looking for them as soon as the sun sets. That is when the males are flying around looking for mates. That's the best time to go on a backyard safari. Bring a friend on safari with you. It will make it easier to capture fireflies.

What Do I Wear?

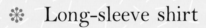

* Long-sleeve shirt
* Jeans or long pants
* A jacket or coat depending on how cold it is

What Do I Take?

* Glass or plastic jar with a lid with holes in it
* Moist paper towel

- ❋ Magnifying glass
- ❋ Flashlight
- ❋ Digital camera
- ❋ Butterfly net
- ❋ Notebook and pencil or pen

Trek Talk

Other names for fireflies are glow flies, moon bugs, and golden sparklers. In Jamaica, they are called blinkies and in Holland, glimworms.

Where Do I Go?

Fireflies will most likely be attracted to these things in your yard:

- ❋ Bushes
- ❋ Moist areas, like around a pond, lake, or stream
- ❋ Vegetable gardens
- ❋ Downed trees, stumps, or logs
- ❋ Wooded areas
- ❋ Grassy areas

This firefly is posed on a blade of grass. Note the glowing light in its abdomen.

If your yard doesn't offer several of these features, here are a few other safari locations you can try:

* Meadows
* Woodlands
* Fields
* Garden nurseries
* Public parks

Make sure to always have an adult with you if you are going beyond your yard. Remember that fireflies are active at night but so are other animals, including raccoons, opossums, and even bats! It's never a good idea to go on a nighttime safari alone.

What Do I Do?

* Use your flashlight to find your way around in the dark. When you see fireflies flashing their lights, use your butterfly net to capture them.

* While one person captures the fireflies with the net, the other

should hold the jar to get the fireflies into it. Beforehand, place the wet paper towel in the jar. This will prevent the jar from drying out and keep the air moist and breathable for the fireflies. Once the fireflies are in the jar, quickly put the lid on to prevent them from escaping.

❋ Catch as many fireflies as you can. See how much light they give off.

❋ Take the jar into a dark room in your house. You may be surprised how much light the fireflies provide. Can you read a book by their light?

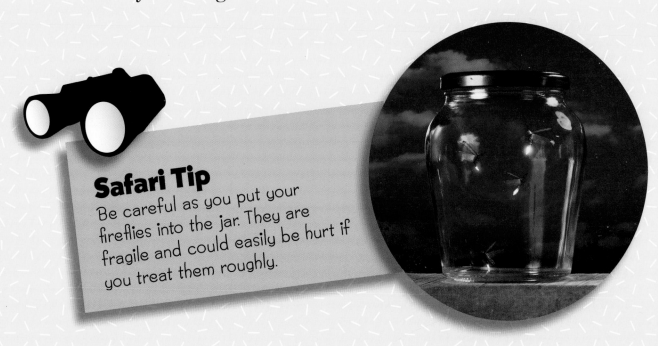

Safari Tip
Be careful as you put your fireflies into the jar. They are fragile and could easily be hurt if you treat them roughly.

What Do I Do Next?

This girl is delighted by the firefly in her hand.

❋ Snap a photo or make a sketch of the fireflies in the jar.

❋ Make a brief entry in your notebook. Try to answer these questions: How many fireflies are in your jar? How long do their flashes last? How many times do they flash in a minute? Are there more than one species in the jar? If so, how do their markings differ? What are they doing in the jar?

❋ Spend about a half hour to one hour on safari.

❋ Release all the fireflies from the jar within a day or two. Otherwise they may die. Be sure to release them at night. This is when they are most active and more likely to escape from predators.

❋ Clean up the area and take everything with you when you leave.

How many fireflies did you see on your safari? How many did you catch? If the answer is none, don't worry. Every safari is different. You are sure to have more success on your next adventure. Plan to go on safari again soon. At home, transfer your photos onto the computer and print them. Now it's time to learn more about your backyard visitors!

THREE
A Guide to Fireflies

About 150 species of fireflies live in the United States and Canada. Here are three of the most common species found in North America.

The Pennsylvania firefly is common through the northeastern United States and Canada. It is about .75 inches (2 cm) in length, is primarily black, and has two red spots on its **thorax**. It is **carnivorous** and eats mostly other insects.

The Winter firefly lives in southeast Canada and throughout the eastern portion of the United States. It is bioluminescent from the larvae stage, but only keeps its light for a few days after becoming an adult

Trek Talk
The Pennsylvania firefly is the official state insect of Pennsylvania.

firefly. Because adults lose their light, males use **pheromones**, or smell signals, to attract females. Unlike other fireflies, the winter firefly, as its name suggests, matures in the winter and early spring. It resides in wooded areas and rests on tree trunks and trees with fresh sap.

The Big Dipper firefly gets its name from the male's odd flight pattern, which has a dipping motion. It lives from South Dakota down to Texas and eastward. This firefly likes open places and grassy areas and flies in a J-pattern. Males in this species have not been observed eating and die quickly after mating.

Of the many foreign fireflies, one of the most fascinating is the Pteroptyx malaccae found in Southeast Asia. They are noted for their blinking lights that resemble Christmas lights. Tourists once came to see thousands of them flashing their lights on the banks of the Mae Klong River near Bangkok, Thailand. In recent years, however, the number of these fireflies has decreased greatly. Like many other firefly species, they are becoming **endangered**.

Winter firefly

Big Dipper firefly

Brimley's Photinus firefly

This so-called Usual Firefly has unusually long antennae.

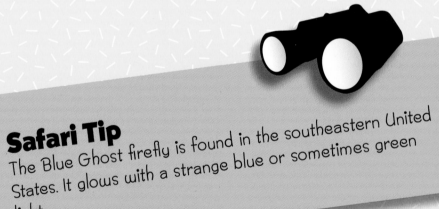

Safari Tip

The Blue Ghost firefly is found in the southeastern United States. It glows with a strange blue or sometimes green light.

Fireflies are Helpful

The chemicals that fireflies produce to make them bioluminescent are useful to people, too. Luciferase can be injected into cells of cancer patients and people with multiple sclerosis, cystic fibrosis, AIDS, and heart disease. The chemical helps detect changes in the cells that may aid scientists one day in curing these diseases. Luciferase has been used in other scientific research. It has even been put into electronic detectors in spacecraft to help identify life in outer space!

Trek Talk
In ancient China, people sometimes captured fireflies in transparent, or clear, containers and used them as lanterns.

Fireflies and Predators

Fireflies can be fierce predators, but most other insect-eating predators leave them alone. When attacked by a predator, fireflies shed drops of blood. The process is known as "reflex bleeding." The blood contains bitter-tasting chemicals that predators don't like. If a predator catches a firefly by mistake, it will often spit it out. If some animals swallow even one firefly, especially reptiles, it can poison and kill them. For this reason, people should never feed their pet snakes or lizards fireflies. While it is not clear how poisonous fireflies are to humans, parents should not allow their children to eat or swallow fireflies.

Fireflies aren't completely safe from predators. This tiger spider, of Costa Rica, has trapped a firefly in its silk.

Although safe from predators, most, if not all, species of fireflies are becoming more and more endangered for other reasons. For example, human development is destroying marshes and wetlands and reducing the fireflies' **habitat**. Also, increased light pollution from buildings and cars and trucks on roadways are confusing firefly light patterns and disrupting mating patterns as well. Finally, the use of chemical pesticides and weed killers on lawns can harm fireflies. Either they come in contact with other insects poisoned by these chemicals or eat plants that have the poison. Preserving habitats, cutting down on light pollution, and reducing the use of pesticides will help save these magical, fascinating glowing insects for future generations.

FOUR

Try This!
Projects You Can Do

Here are three projects you can do with fireflies. Be sure to get a friend or family member to help you with them.

"Talking" With Fireflies

Every species of firefly has its own unique flashing or blinking light pattern it gives off to attract mates of the same species. You can try to "talk" their light language and learn about different species by imitating their flashing patterns. You can also use this project to capture more fireflies by attracting them to your light!

What Do I Need?

✿ A penlight with a sensitive switch

✿ A blue disc or cut piece of paper

✿ A notebook and pencil or pen

✿ Jar with a lid that has holes in it

✿ Butterfly net

What Do I Do?

✿ Place the blue disc or piece of paper over the front of your penlight. This will produce a blue light that will not confuse the fireflies like white lights might.

✿ Observe the flash patterns of a firefly in your yard. Then try to duplicate the pattern with your penlight. Aim the penlight downward from your chest so the firefly can see it clearly.

✿ If the firefly responds and flies toward you, use your net to capture it and then transfer it into the jar.

✿ Don't be discouraged if your signals don't work immediately. Keep trying. See if you observe different patterns from different species and try to match each one.

✿ Make an entry in your notebook about each different light pattern you see a firefly make. What color was it? How many flashes or blinks? How much time passed between flashes? Did the firefly respond to the flashes from your penlight?

FIREFLY	
Color of Light: Green	
Number of Flashes: Two long, one short	
Duration Between Them: About a second	
How It Responded: Flew towards my light and I caught it.	

Remember to follow the same steps you did in Chapter 2 when you captured your fireflies.

Making A "Firefly Friendly" Corner in Your Backyard

As we said in Chapter 3, fireflies are disappearing and may be becoming an endangered species. There are ways you can make your backyard a haven for fireflies and increase their numbers in your neighborhood.

What Do I Need?

* A shovel
* Water source (a garden hose)
* Some deadwood or logs
* A lawnmower
* A notebook and pen or pencil

What Do I Do?

* Pick one area of your backyard to be your firefly friendly corner. You might want to make it the farthest part of your backyard from your house so the least light from your house reaches it.

You can study fireflies up close when you catch them in a jar.

* When you mow your lawn, leave the grass uncut in this corner. Fireflies like to congregate in tall grass.

* Scatter some deadwood or logs in your corner, especially under trees. Firefly larvae thrive in deadwood.

* Take your shovel and dig a small hole or depression in one part of your firefly corner. Fill it with water from the hose. Fireflies like water and wet areas. If you have a stream on your

property, see if you can divert it by digging a trench to your firefly corner. Make sure you have permission from your parents or guardians and get them to help you. This could be a great family project!

* After you have finished creating your firefly friendly corner, visit it nightly. Do you notice more fireflies there now than previously? Are there more fireflies in your corner than in the rest of your backyard? Try to count the fireflies by observing their light flashes and keep a running tally in your notebook.

* Tell your neighbors about your firefly friendly corner and encourage them to try creating one of their own. You can help them get started.

This firefly in flight may be searching for a mate.

Report Your Firefly Sightings

The Boston Museum of Science has an ongoing firefly project. It is asking people all across the country to report on firefly sightings in their yards. It is using this data to better understand firefly mating patterns and the population of fireflies in the United States.

You can become a part of this important project that could help to save these endangered insects.

What Do I Do?

* Go to the Boston Museum of Science website at: legacy.mos.org/fireflywatch/

* Register to join the firefly project, and then log in.

* Provide a description of your study site (your backyard).

* Fill out an observation sheet each time you visit your backyard to look for fireflies. Fill it out even if you see no fireflies on a visit. The museum wants to know this, too.

* On the website, you can visit a virtual habitat, learn more about the project, and join an online discussion board.

Take pride in knowing you have done your part to help save these fascinating flashy beetles in these projects. And enjoy your time on safari with them!

Glossary

abdomen   the rear part of the body of many insects

beetles   insects with hard outer forewings that protect the flying wings

bioluminescence   the glowing light produced by fireflies and some other insects

carnivorous   eating the flesh of animals

elytra   the hard outer wings of a beetle

endangered   an animal or other living thing that is threatened with extinction

enzyme   a protein that can produce chemical changes in living things

habitat   the natural environment where an insect or animal lives

larvae   the wingless, wormlike stage of some insects

mate   to partner with another animal for purposes of reproduction

pheromones   chemical substances released by an animal or insect to influence the behavior of another member of the same species

predators	animals that naturally prey (hunt) on other animals for food
prey	animals that predators hunt and eat
pupa	an insect in the nonfeeding, often immobile stage between larva and adult
species	one type of animal within a larger category
thorax	the part of an insect's body between the head and the abdomen

Find Out More

Books

Bryant, Megan E. *Fireflies.* New York: Penguin Young Readers, 2008.

Dunn, Mary Rose. *Fireflies.* Pebble Plus: Nocturnal Animals. Mankato, MN: Capstone Press, 2011.

Hall, Margaret. *Fireflies.* Bugs Bugs Bugs. Mankato, MN: Capstone Press, 2006.

Websites

Firefly

firefly.org

Learn many fascinating facts about fireflies, why they are endangered, and how to catch them.

National Children's Museum: Ready, Set, Glow

readysetglow.org

Learn about how to help save the endangered firefly, play a firefly game, and read jokes about fireflies.

Surprising Science: 14 Fun Facts About Fireflies

blogs.smithsonianmag.com/science/2012/06/14-fun-facts-about-fireflies/

Discover interesting information about fireflies and see a close-up photograph of a firefly.

Index

Page numbers in **boldface** are illustrations.

abdomen, 8, **12**

beetles, 5, 8, 27
Big Dipper firefly, 16, **17**
bioluminescence, 8

carnivorous, 15

elytra, 8
endangered, 16, 21, 24, 27
enzyme, 8

glowworm, 7

habitat, 21,
    preserving habitats, 21
    virtual habitat, 27

larvae, 6, 7, 15, 25
    appetite, 7
    eggs become larvae, 6
life span, 7
lightening bugs, 5, **6**

mate, 6, 7, **7**, **8**, 9, 10, 22, **26**
mating patterns, 21, 27

Pennsylvania firefly, 15, **15**
pheromones, 16
predators, 8, 14, 20, **20**, 21
prey, 7
    see also predators
pupa, 7

reflex bleeding, 20

species, 6, 7, 9, 14
    see also Big Dipper
       firefly; Pennsylvania
       firefly; Winter firefly

thorax, 15

Winter firefly, 15, **17**

About the Author

Steven Otfinoski has written more than 150 books for young readers, including many about animals ranging from koalas to scorpions. He lives in Connecticut with his wife, their daughter, and two dogs.